teach me about

Tasting

Copyright © Joy Berry, 2022
Originally Published, 1986

All rights are reserved.

No part of this book can be duplicated or used without the prior written permission of the copyright owner, except for the use of brief quotations from the book.

For inquiries or permission requests contact the publisher.

Published by Joy Berry Enterprises
www.joyberryenterprises.com

teach me about

By JOY BERRY

Illustrated by Bartholomew

I have a mouth.

There is a tongue in my mouth.

My tongue helps me to taste

the things I put into my mouth.

Some things I put in my mouth have a **sweet** taste.

Some things I put

in my mouth

have a **sour** taste.

Some things I put

in my mouth

have a **salty** taste.

Some things I put

in my mouth

have a **bitter** taste.

There are teeth inside my mouth. My teeth help me to chew things. They also help me to feel the texture of the things I put into my mouth.

Some things I chew have a **hard** texture.

Some things I chew have a **soft** texture.

Some things I chew have a **crisp** texture.

Some things I chew have a **chewy** texture.

The inside of my mouth can feel the **temperature** of things.

It can feel how hot or cold things are.

The temperature of some things

I put into my mouth is **hot**.

The temperature of some things

I put into my mouth is **cold**.

The temperature of some things I put in my mouth is **warm**.

There are many different kinds of food.

Each food has its own
- taste,
- texture, and
- temperature.

There are some foods

I do not like to taste.

There are some foods

I like to taste.

helpful hints for parents about

Dear Parents:

The purpose of this book is
- to define the purpose of the mouth in regard to a child's gustatory perception of the world, and
- to help children develop the sensory awareness that is fundamental to all learning.

You can best implement the purpose of this book by
- reading it to your child, and
- reading the following *Helpful Hints* and using them whenever applicable.

INFANT TASTES

Preferences

Infant tastes are highly discriminating. Newborn taste buds are very sensitive, and infants show a preference for the tastes of some liquids over others. Once a sweetener has been introduced into liquids, such as water, most babies refuse to accept the plain variety again.

Stimulate taste buds slowly

Breast milk or formula supplemented by plain water will satisfy the nutritional needs of most babies for the first four months. Unless your baby's health practitioner recommends otherwise, avoid introducing solid foods or sweetened liquids to your baby under five months old. This precaution guarantees a better nutritional start as well as providing some protection against food allergies. Flexibility in the feeding routine is good for baby and parents. Babies who are breast-fed exclusively may resist a bottle, making mother's availability essential to mealtime. Here are some ways to make feedings more flexible:

- Introduce a bottle to your breast-fed baby as a supplement. An occasional bottle not only gives the mother a break, but offers an opportunity for fathers and other family members to share in feeding the baby.
- Allow fathers and family members to share in the feeding of the formula-fed baby.
- Offer your baby water in a bottle between feedings, especially during hot weather.
- Try a variety of nipples and bottles on a baby who initially refuses a bottle.
- Offer a pacifier between feedings in the early months to satisfy your baby's sucking urge. Some babies have no use for them while others seem to suck during all of their waking hours.

DEVELOPMENTAL READINESS AND EATING

A baby's first year is a time of dramatic changes in growth and development. Proper nutrition is essential to maximum growth. Physical development will determine what kinds of foods your baby will eat and how he or she will eat them. Babies are individuals growing at different rates. The following guidelines *suggest* appropriate foods, amounts, and feeding skills in baby's first year:

Age	Physical Development	Foods/Daily
Birth to four months	Sucking and swallowing on reflex; by four months, controlled sucking; early eye and head control; no solid foods necessary.	Breast milk or formula on demand or every three to four hours;
Five to six months	Able to grasp and sit up with support; tongue control for taking solids from a spoon.	Breast milk or formula on demand or every four hours; cereal mixed with above; two feedings, 3-5 Tbs.
Seven to eight months	Side-to-side tongue control for chewing semisoft foods; teething begins; head, hand, and body coordination improve; holds cup or bottle.	Breast milk or formula; ½ cup cereal; 6 oz. fruits/vegetables (strained or blended).
Nine months	Grasps finger foods; improved hand-to-mouth coordination; capable of feeding self soft table foods as finger food.	Breast milk or formula (1 qt.); ½ cup cereal; ½-1 cup fruits/vegetables; ½ oz. (2 Tbs.) meat, poultry, fish, cheese, yogurt, legumes; finger foods such as dry cereal, cooked vegetable strips, peeled soft fruit, small cheese chunks.

Age	Physical Development	Foods/Daily
Ten to twelve months	Capable of feeding self with a spoon; holds and drinks from a cup.	Breast milk, formula, or fresh whole milk (1 qt.); ½-¾ cup cereal; ½ cup each of table foods including cooked vegetables, fruits, meats/cheese, potatoes, noodles (mashed or chopped); finger foods.
One year	Steady improvement at feeding self with spoon and cup, but may prefer finger feeding.	All food groups including fresh whole milk and whole egg if no apparent allergy; fortified cereal; may be weaned from breast or bottle.

At one year old your baby has established a foundation of good nutrition from a variety of foods. The adventure of good eating and new tastes has just begun.

Exploring new tastes

Toddlers are natural explorers and their sense of adventure can be applied to mealtimes as well. New foods that are presented and tasted enthusiastically by the whole family are generally a hit with the youngest members, too. Here are a few suggestions for introducing a new food to your toddler:
- Present the food attractively in a form the child is used to eating on his or her own. For example, serve steamed broccoli flowerets as finger food.
- Serve foods separately rather than in a stew or casserole. Children like to examine and taste each food item separately.
- Offer a food that has been rejected in a different form at a later date.
- Change the texture of a rejected food if possible. For example, a vegetable in a gelatin square or in a semifrozen state may be more palatable than steamed or boiled.

- Encourage, but don't force, a new taste experience. A finicky eater can grow into a gourmet with opportunity and encouragement.
- Ask your child to describe the texture of a new food before describing it yourself. Discuss the difference between how a food tastes and how it feels in the mouth.
- Serve the same food in two or three different forms and ask your child's preference, if any. For example, serve carrots grated raw, in steamed slices, and cooked and mashed.
- Keep new food as close to natural as possible. Cook as necessary but avoid condiments, fats, salt, and spices.
- Avoid using food to influence your child's behavior.

A HEALTHY MOUTH

For about the first year babies use their mouths to experience their world. The mouth is used as finger tips to feel the textures of objects and surfaces. Whatever goes into the hand goes directly into the mouth.

Common problems

Choking is a common occurrence for babies learning to feed themselves and for those sampling the many inedible parts of their environment. Choking or gagging is a reflex action which protects babies from inhaling or swallowing large chunks of food or foreign objects. If food or an object seems lodged in your baby's throat, turn the baby upside down and pat him or her firmly on the back. If the baby continues to choke, call or send someone to call for emergency medical aid while you continue the procedure. If your baby begins wheezing after a choking episode, it could indicate the presence of a small foreign object in the lungs. If you suspect that this has happened, have your baby checked by a doctor.

Pica is an eating disorder in which children eat abnormal substances, such as ashes, paint chips, and soil. Very young children experiment with eating whatever is in the environment. In the case of pica, however, there seems to

be a desire to consume a particular substance that could be related to a nutritional deficiency, and the child should be checked by a physician.
Nursing bottle syndrome affects the teeth of young children who take bottles to bed and fall asleep with them in their mouths. This can lead to dental caries and early tooth loss. Have your child's teeth examined by a dentist before the age of three.
Thrush is a fungus infection of the mouth usually occurring in young infants. White patches appearing on the inside of cheeks, on the tongue, and on lips may indicate thrush. Consult your child's doctor for a diagnosis and prescription.
Upper respiratory infections can cause mouth problems. When mouth breathing becomes necessary because of a stuffy nose, the mouth can become dry and subject to viral infections such as *canker and cold sores* (fever blisters). *Chapped lips* can also result from mouth breathing or exposure to dry air. All of the above conditions are treatable with over-the-counter pharmaceuticals or home remedies. Consult your child's physician in the case of complications.

Teeth
Dental care should begin with the appearance of your child's first tooth. Use the following schedule of care for your child's teeth:

- *First year*—Clean baby's teeth daily with a clean cloth or gauze.
- *One to two years old*—Brush child's teeth daily with a soft toothbrush. Encourage your child to brush his or her own teeth as well.
- *Two to three years old*—Brush and floss your child's teeth daily. Emphasize brushing after eating. Let your child brush on his or her own. Take your child to the dentist for the first time. Limit sugars in your child's diet.
- *Three to six years old*—Help your child brush and floss on his or her own. Limit sugars in your child's diet. Encourage brushing after eating. Take your child to the dentist twice a year.

TASTE EXPERIENCES

Encourage your child to experiment with new tastes and to experience the characteristics of a variety of tastes.

Use a vocabulary of taste with your child when you describe different tastes.

Distinguish the various categories of taste such as sweet, sour, salty, and bitter.

Characterize the texture of foods by calling attention to hard, soft, chewy, and crisp textures.

Ask your child to note the temperature of what he or she is eating.

Experiment with the preparation of foods that fit into a category of taste. The following foods are appropriate for tasting experience and are not nutritionally superior. Avoid giving popcorn, nuts, and seeds to children under three. Here are some examples of taste categories:

- *sweet tastes*—fruit juice drinks, yogurt popsicles, cookies, fruit combinations, peanut butter candies, ice cream, pudding.
- *sour tastes*—lemonade, lemon tarts, deviled eggs, sauerkraut, sourdough bread, dill pickles.
- *salty tastes*—nuts, french fried potatoes, potato chips, corn chips, bacon, lunch meats, cheeses, popcorn, roasted pumpkin seeds, roasted sunflower seeds.
- *bitter tastes* (this taste is not generally favored)— Kool-aid without sugar, pimento stuffed olives, cucumbers and radishes, cooked brussel sprouts.

www.ingramcontent.com/pod-product-compliance
Lightning Source LLC
Chambersburg PA
CBHW081410070526
44583CB00020B/2747